SHIT,
I Got Fired

························

*A short, no B.S. guide on how to
get hired after being unexpectedly fired*

DICK BARLIK

Print ISBN: 978-1-54398-159-9

eBook ISBN: 978-1-54398-160-5

CONTENTS

FOREWORD

This book is for you. I am not here to give you fluffy motivational advice that leaves you inspired, but without direction. I trust that you are already inspired enough to pursue your next job and that you need some real advice to follow. This book includes actual actions you can take in order to go from being unexpectedly fired to successfully hired. It is advice I have gathered from my own successes and failures. This advice has already helped others land their next job after getting fired. I have tried to keep it short and clear because I imagine the last thing you want to read right now is a long, dense book. Before you take any action on your job search, take a few hours to finish this. A few simple tips may shorten your transition period by several months.

INTRODUCTION

Getting fired sucks. Getting fired blows. Getting fired can be the fucking worst. Getting fired can also be the best (looking backward).

This book was written just for you, the guy or gal who just got fired. I've gotten fired before, and look at me now—I'm an author!

Just kidding. I found a job after I got fired, and then I thought I would write a book for others who could benefit from all the special knowledge I gained throughout the process, knowledge that will help you endure the "just got fired" phase and help you land your next job.

Don't worry—this isn't another soft-spoken self-help book written by some washed-out maniac who claims to be a "life coach" after forty years of never discovering what they want to do. It is not written by someone who has never had to utilize public transportation. This book will not just leave you passively motivated, but rather will give you a set of actionable steps that will take you where you want to go. If you are reading this and you just got fired as a life coach, it is likely that you were self-employed, and you fired yourself. You can skip the remainder of the book and rehire yourself now.

Regardless of the industry in which you work, or seek to work, the contents of this book will be relevant to you. It will be applicable to you whether you are looking for a blue-collar job or a white-collar job. The advice that follows will also be relevant to you regardless of age, sex, or any other demographic factor.

I am not going to go into great detail about my life—that would be a complete waste of your time (and mine, since I had to talk about myself way too much during the interview process). However, I am sure you want to know enough about me to be comfortable taking my advice.

I am from Philadelphia. I graduated college, and I have an MBA. For all of you who are thinking, "Of course this guy got a new job; he has an MBA," you need to abandon this thinking. You and I both have plenty of peers who are doing way better than us and yet have less "formal" education. I was on the recruiting team at a very large and well-known company, and no hiring decision ever came down to where someone earned their degree or whether they had a graduate school education.

While in college, I landed a few internships, and then received an offer for my first full time position before I graduated. I went to graduate school, where I earned internships during the school year and over the summer. While still in graduate school, I landed another full-time position. Throughout my career, I have been a decent performer and have had a solid reputation. I have worked in different industries and found that there are some things that stay consistent across all of them in terms of landing the job. I worked at my most recent full-time position for about four years until I was abruptly fired. If you are interested in knowing more about my background, please visit my LinkedIn page or send me an email (SIGFmarc@gmail.com).

This is the part where I help you. I recently landed my next full-time job, and I want to help you land yours. It was important for me to write everything down that got me here so I could share it with you. Priceless little nuggets of advice are what you will find in the following pages.

I know right now you might be feeling a little salty or bitter, but please listen to my advice and follow my instructions. Some of my advice may seem very simple, and you may question it at first, but trust me, you will be surprised by its effectiveness. Before you read on, turn your phone off, take a big breath in through your nose, and exhale slowly.

It is important for me to let you know my agenda in writing this book. I have some time off before my new job starts, and I feel like I have a tremendous and fulfilling opportunity to help a wide range of people by sharing effective advice backed by personal experience. If I am fortunate, I may get the added benefit of selling copies of this book to people beyond my immediately family. Nothing would make me happier than to receive thank-you emails from people who have read this, telling me about how it helped them and where they are headed next.

CHAPTER 1

What's Likely To Be Going Through Your Head Right Now...

Fuck them!

Ugh!

What am I going to do now?

I knew I should have started looking sooner while I was still there!

This is so unfair!

I never thought this would happen to me!

I can't believe I got fired and Tyler didn't!

What about all those plans I made that assumed I would still have a job?

What am I going to tell my spouse?

What am I going to tell my family?

My dog is going to be able to tell.

Perhaps some of this sounds like you, perhaps not. Maybe you sound more like...

Thank God.

I was waiting for that.

I'm free!

I had a feeling that was going to happen.

I needed that.

Either way, there is a lot going on in your head right now, and your thoughts are likely traveling rapidly.

The first thing you need to acknowledge is that this is completely normal, and that there is no need to make any conclusions about your thoughts any time soon. The most important thing is to simply be aware of what you're thinking about and try to pick up on the thoughts that stick around over the course of the next few days, weeks, or months while you are unemployed. It is likely that you will be very emotional immediately after getting fired, and we all know how bad things can get when we let our emotions take over our decision-making process. The point of not making any conclusions about your thoughts today is to let those emotions cool off and to start thinking more rationally. Don't take action on anything yet. Don't start applying to jobs when you get home or calling the first job opportunity that comes to mind. Also, do not publicly bash your former company or colleagues. Do not say anything about them or your experience on social media. If you want to say anything negative about your employer, experience, or colleagues, do not put it in writing, even if it is discussed between you and a personal friend. Trust me. It is very important not to burn bridges or put yourself in an even worse position.

First instruction: take a thirty-minute walk and either turn your phone off or do not bring it with you at all. Don't listen to music as you walk, and don't walk with anyone. Go alone and let the only attendees on your walk be you and your thoughts. Read on when you return.

Welcome back. Think about which thoughts popped up most often, as well as which feelings you felt. Ask yourself: What message could those thoughts and feelings be sending you?

For example, if you are feeling a sense of relief, maybe getting fired was the final thing you needed to confirm that you actually did not enjoy the work you were doing. That is a huge positive and is helping to point you in the right direction.

If you can't stop thinking about how unfair it was that you got fired, and you're bitter, just remember that it is what it is and there is not much you can do about it. It's highly unlikely your previous employer will take you back, and if they do, it is going to be very awkward for everyone. What happened, happened. Think more about what you're going to do next instead of looking backward.

If you want to sue your previous employer for wrongful termination, just remember that you are possibly suing a person or entity that, relative to you, has unlimited time, money, patience, and legal resources to fight you. If you start a fight, you lose the opportunity to work toward your next job, and your level of stress will increase exponentially.

Perhaps you are embarrassed and concerned about what others will think about you. That is completely natural, and that is how most people will feel when they get fired. Remember right now that you don't have to figure out a way to *not* feel that way; you just have to accept it and know that it will not last forever. Take another deep breath—more people have been in your shoes than you realize. Tens of thousands of people are fired each day for a multitude of reasons, so you are not alone.

CHAPTER 2

The Very First Things You Should Do

You leave your office, and now you are free. Wow. What the hell is going on?

Even though you just lost your job, the rest of your life is still in motion. You still owe your monthly rent or mortgage payment. You still have your other bills to pay. You still have lunches, non-business meetings, and other occasions sitting on your calendar. You still have to buy diapers (hopefully not for yourself). You have wedding and birthday gifts to buy for people. To make sure your typical life operations do not get in the way of your job hunt, you must get organized.

I used to run my entire life through my work calendar. If I had lunch scheduled with my friend, it was on my work calendar. If I had a plumber visit scheduled for Friday at my apartment, it was on my work calendar. If I had a reminder to call my brother on Tuesday night at 6 p.m., it was on my work calendar. If I had a trip planned two months from now, it was on my work calendar, along with flight information. With this being said, the first thing you should do when you get home is update your calendar. It is essential to get organized and maintain your sanity. This is especially important if you will no longer have access to your work email. Gmail has a great calendar that is easy to use. If you are old-school and prefer a paper calendar, go for it. If you not only are recently fired, but also start missing appointments because you failed to organize your life after getting fired, the people in your life will start to think you getting fired makes sense. If people are not surprised you got fired, they will be less likely to introduce you to potential future employers. Being disorganized in your personal life while you are hunting for the next opportunity may even make you doubt yourself. Organize your calendar with every single thing you are aware will be coming up in the next few months.

Once your calendar is fully up to date with all appointments and reminders, clean your home. Whether you own a house, rent an apartment, or simply occupy a room, make sure to clean it thoroughly and reduce clutter. How much more stressful do you think it will be to embark on a job search if you are sitting in a chair surrounded by trash, dirty dishes, and other non-essentials? This goes for not only your desk area, but also your bedroom, bathroom, and any other living spaces. Remember: How you do one thing is usually how you do everything. If your living space is chaotic, you can expect your job search to be chaotic as well.

Speaking of cleaning up, deactivate all your social media accounts except for LinkedIn. But before you do so, clean them up by deleting any content you wouldn't want a future employer to see. Oh, you're not worried, because your account is private? They will find a way to see it if they want to see it. It's 2019. Just do it. There is no reason whatsoever to use Instagram during this time unless it somehow provides you with income. If you absolutely must use Instagram because you are so addicted that you will die if you can't open it, create a separate account and only follow accounts that provide you with motivational fuel (try @ thegoodquote for starters). Deactivate your main account. You're not missing out on anything other than some pictures of your friend's trip to the Bahamas (she actually fought with her boyfriend the whole time, but the picture they posted looks great) or some shitty picture of your other friend's avocado toast.

If LinkedIn is completely irrelevant to your industry, skip the next paragraph.

On LinkedIn, make sure you update your account and click the button that lets employers and recruiters know you are actively looking for a new position. You can find exact instructions on this by going to Google and searching *How to let recruiters know on LinkedIn*. There are many useful (and free) guides online that detail how to strengthen your profile. Are you mad because I'm not writing out all the steps to creating a perfect LinkedIn profile? You should thank me for what I am about to say next: do not buy an entire book that instructs you on how to create a perfect LinkedIn profile. The online resources I mentioned are unlimited and sufficient. If you buy a book, you will just be wasting a ton of time (and money) perfecting a LinkedIn profile when you could be finding more job opportunities.

If you will be doing most of your emailing, calling, and researching from home during this time, make sure you are doing it from a part of your home that is comfortable and not gloomy. If you feel you will be most productive doing everything from your bed, go for it! If your desk is in a dark place, pull it right up next to a window so you can remember there is an entire world out there that is yours to take.

Even if you plan to do most of your activity from home, you absolutely must change your scenery at least one or two days per week. Perhaps the best environment for you is outside your home every single day that you are on your search. For example, take your computer, cell phone, notepad, and chargers to a coffee shop (with Wi-Fi) and work from there. What you will discover is that there are a lot of people just like you who are on their grind, either as entrepreneurs or as people trying to make that next move.

As mentioned, once you get fired, it does not mean your monthly expenses will cease to exist. Thus, you suddenly must think more carefully about all those monthly bills you were paying without really thinking. If it is not something you have done already, count up all the money you have access to right now, and then add up all the expenses you will have over the next few months. You can use whatever time period you think is relevant. You can make a very simple chart like the one below. I also have a blank one available on my website for you to use:

www.ShitIGotFired.com

Bills to Cover - September 2020					
Sources of $			Bills to Pay		
Account	Amount		Item	Amount	Due Date
Citibank (checking)	$ 2,000.00		Mortgage Payment	$ 700.00	9/8/20
Bank of America (savings)	$ 4,000.00		Cell Phone Bill	$ 100.00	9/14/20
Investment Account	$ 7,000.00		Electric Bill	$ 80.00	9/20/20
Item:	$ -		Car Payment	$ 250.00	9/25/20
Item:	$ -		Health Insurance	$ 400.00	9/26/20
Item:	$ -		Car Insurance	$ 100.00	9/29/20
Item:	$ -		Item:	$ -	
Item:	$ -		Item:	$ -	
Item:	$ -		Item:	$ -	
Item:	$ -		Item:	$ -	
Item:	$ -		Item:	$ -	
Total Available	$ 13,000.00		Total Due	$ 1,630.00	

I have no idea what your financial situation is, so I cannot dive too deeply into this. Illustrating this will help you anticipate future expenses and have the necessary funds lined up to pay them. The last thing you want to do while you are unemployed and making less money than you were before is fight with the bank over massive overdraft fees levied because you forgot to transfer money into your account. Do not get blindsided as a result of poor preparation and not mapping things out for yourself.

It is possible your employer provided you with a severance package after you were fired. There should be a telephone number you can call to speak with the individuals managing your severance and the associated benefits. I do not know this telephone number, because it is different for each employer. Call to get a thorough understanding of what exactly your benefits are (health insurance, dental insurance, etc.) and how long they will last. Weigh your options and update your budget worksheet to reflect this information.

One thing that also does not stop once you get fired is your hunger. After you get fired, you will have so much on your mind that the last thing you will want to think about is what you are going to eat at each meal. Take a trip to the grocery store and get food for the upcoming week. Pre-cook all your meals on one day (or get meals that are very easy to prepare) so you are not spending your valuable time and headspace on eating decisions. Eat as healthy as you can.

Now you have created an environment for yourself that is facilitative to your finding the next opportunity more efficiently and less stressfully.

CHAPTER 3

Figuring Out What It Is You Want To Do Next In Terms Of Your Career

I am going to try my best to not get too life coach-y on you in this chapter. My advice here is simple but difficult to follow because you have to push away pressures that you are allowing to conquer you.

You absolutely must trust your gut at this stage. As you think about what you want to do next, you have to determine into which of the following categories it fits:

Is it something that you are pursuing because...

...others think you would be good at doing it?

...others have made a lot of money doing it?

...others have told you to do it?

...you are passionate about it?

...you think it would be fulfilling?

...you think it would be interesting?

...it may not be your end goal, but it will help you get to it?

...you think people would be proud of you for doing it?

…you would get a lot of pleasure out of it purely because of the title or prestige it carries?

Four of the above are the only ones that matter. I am pretty sure you can guess which ones. All that matters is whether this next opportunity is something you are passionate about, you think would be fulfilling, you think would be interesting, and which may not be your end goal, but may help you get there.

There are way too many variables at play here for a wide reader base. If you are undecided about whether to launch a startup you've always wanted to build, I can't help you. I am here to help you land your next job. I do not know your financial, family, or health situations, and I know they may play into your decision. For this reason, some additional questions you may want to ask yourself are as follows:

Are you more interested in high potential earnings with a higher risk of losing your job (typically sales- and/or performance-based positions) or a lower salary with more security?

Are you more interested in gaining the skill set and experience you will need in a future role, or in having the brand name of the company at which you intend to work on your resume (there are opportunities where you can get both)?

Are you trying to take the path of least resistance and transfer into a position that is as similar as possible to your previous position and/or skill set?

I encourage you to think backward from your future goals— think five to ten years down the road. Ask yourself the following:

Is it your goal to be making $XXX,XXX annually by a certain age?

Is it your goal to have a skill set that you can take to any city and have a high likelihood of getting a job there?

I don't have the answers to any of these questions for you, because I am not you. Think about them while asking yourself whether the job opportunities you are considering are going to help you get there. If they do not meet your requirements, or if they will not help you achieve those goals, eliminate them from your mind and do not spend one more ounce of your energy or one more second of your time thinking about them. This will help you narrow down your options and stay focused.

CHAPTER 4

How To Treat Your Body After You Get Fired

If you want to stay sane throughout this process, you have to treat your body the right way. Physical health translates into mental health. I am not going to waste your time citing the thousands of academic research pieces that support this statement.

If you had a regular workout routine while you were still employed, you absolutely must make sure to not break that routine. A huge mistake many recently fired employees make is thinking they must dedicate 100 percent of their time to the job hunt and ditch the workout routine.

Do not punish yourself like that—this course of action will actually lead to the opposite of the desired effect. An employer will have a more positive perception of the work you may eventually do for them if they see you are capable of taking care of yourself. Your workouts will also generate many of the naturally created drugs (endorphins, dopamine, etc.) in your body that elevate your mood and thus elevate your confidence, which will be crucial as you fill out applications, make phone calls, compose emails, and interview. With the additional time in your schedule, it might even be a good idea to add workouts to your calendar. You would be hurting yourself more than helping yourself by missing your workouts. Try your best to do something every day, even if it is just for twenty minutes. You have the time, and you know it. Put it on your calendar!

If you did not get regular physical activity in while you were employed, don't worry—I am not going to instruct you to transform into a globally recognized triathlete. Rather, I suggest doing something physical every day that is extremely manageable, be it a light jog, a long walk, biking, swimming, yoga, or a couple sets of pushups. You will be baffled by the amount of headspace and mental clarity that the activity will open up for you.

Outside of your regularly scheduled workouts, make sure to take plenty of opportunities to walk around the block or just sit outside to reflect on your efforts and what you want. Turn off your cell phone for the duration of these contemplative periods, or just do not bring it with you at all! Of course, only completely turn off your phone or leave it at home if it does not put you in a less safe position. If you do not like the idea of completely turning off your phone or leaving it at home, bring it with you and put it on mute. If this is still too risky for you, then at the very least make a concerted effort to not check it frequently.

Everyone needs sleep, but the amount of sleep that leads to optimal performance varies from person to person. We've all talked about that threshold before, right? That number of hours of sleep that you need or else you are in stupid mode throughout the day. For me, that amount of sleep is seven hours. I have learned over time that if I get at least a full seven hours of sleep, I think clearly, I am able to speak articulately and without stuttering, my memory retention is solid, I am more focused, I maintain better eye contact, I feel less anxious, and I don't get tired in the middle of the day. Do not think for a second that you can compensate for this by drinking coffee. Coffee and other stimulants, when you go below your threshold, are likely to just exaggerate all the typical side effects of your lack of sleep. There is no substitute for sleep. Getting that additional hour of sleep may enable you to cut down on the time it takes to complete your tasks throughout the day. You get it—know your threshold and never go below it.

There is one final thing you should do that is small but helpful. After you silence your alarm clock in the morning, do not look at your phone for at least the first five minutes of wakefulness. The five-minute period that starts when you wake up is prime time to take note of the thoughts that are top of mind and to gauge if you are still feeling the same way about things you were excited about or that were bothering you in the days prior. That recruiter who reached out to you on LinkedIn about that job you never considered before might be your first thought. You may realize that for several days you haven't even thought about that other opportunity for which everyone has been telling you that you would be the perfect fit. Looking at your phone before you have any chance to think for yourself is essentially asking your phone to tell you what you should be thinking about right now. You can wait as long as you would like to look at your phone. One rule I play by personally is that I don't look at my phone until I figure out what it is that I want from it. I don't just let a feeling of anxiety or worry force me to pick up my phone to look for comfort or distraction, and you shouldn't either.

CHAPTER 5

Be Selfish As F*ck

This is the time to be very selfish with your time. If you were a sucker when it came to accepting invitations to social events (happy hours, parties, etc.) while you were still working, you can't be a sucker anymore.

Aside from your workouts or reflective time outside, it is completely acceptable to be 100 percent focused on your job search. While I was unemployed, I would describe myself as a bit of a hermit to my friends. I told them I would be this way until the dust settled with my job pursuit. If your friends abandon you for taking this attitude, or reject you for your admirable discipline, they are not great friends.

With this being said, I am not recommending you skip every social gathering to which you are invited (they can be great opportunities to network your way into your next position). It is OK to go briefly simply for the sake of making an appearance and then leave early. If all you will be thinking about while you are out splurging on social activities is your job search, and if it will make you miserable, don't go at all or cut your time short. Stay at home and dominate your job search with full force. However, if the social gatherings are full of people who may be helpful in your career pursuit, it may make sense to stay.

If you tend to be a caring person who makes a lot of time for others, it is OK to cut back on your hangouts and phone conversations or skip them altogether. It is very difficult to feed others if you can't even feed yourself. Perhaps try to set time limits on your conversations or activities (e.g., "I will call my brother to see how his weekend was, but I will politely end the conversation after seven minutes") so that you don't find yourself saying, "Where did the time go today?" Make sure to let them know that you care about them, but also that you are focused on your job search and will thus be a little less communicative while you are closing in on that next job.

Be selfish with your money. Your cash-flow spigot just got completely turned off. Unless you have other sources of income, you are bleeding. Cut your expenses down to the essentials, but feel free to continue to spend occasionally on things that will help you de-stress, whether it is a yoga class, a stimulating lecture, a kayak rental, or an overpriced pumpkin spice chai tea latte cappuccino with a splash of soy milk and coconut-milk foam from Starbucks.

If you have an extremely significant amount of savings or generate cash flow from other business interests, you are fortunate, but perhaps you can be less stringent. Even if you do have significant backup funds, it may be helpful to cut down your spending a little simply to serve as a reminder that your main priority is finding your next opportunity.

You will be tempted to participate in activities that you know deep down will be counterproductive to your job pursuit. Push them away and remember your goal.

CHAPTER 6

The Best Attitude For A Smooth Transition

Attitude is everything, right? That's what all those super-accomplished life coaches and fluffy self-help books tell you.

They're partially right. Of course, attitude is only part of the equation. You can't just sit at home in your underwear shadowboxing on your couch while screaming "RA-RA!" as you play reruns of Tony Robbins and Gary Vaynerchuk videos. Attitude combined with careful execution of the new job conquest strategies covered in the next few chapters is what will get you that offer.

If you allow abundant rejection throughout the job-search process to bring you down and make you question your own value, you will begin to subconsciously present yourself as a less valuable asset to people you meet. If you are chasing something great, it is inevitable that you will get rejected quite a bit, and that is completely fine. Make sure to never dilute that perception of your own worth that you had when you were dismissed. You are fully capable of landing your next job soon, and this process will not last forever. Let me reiterate that you are going to get rejected a lot. Take whatever your idea of getting rejected "a lot" is and anticipate getting rejected even more than that. That is likely still less than you will actually be rejected. It's part of the journey.

Take in a deep breath through your nose and exhale slowly.

You're probably feeling a lot of things right now. Totally normal. There are a lot of motivational quotes out there, and I am not going to list any of them here. The only language I speak in my world is reality. Instead of motivational quotes provided by "Certified Life Coaches," here is some real talk to keep in mind as you go through this process:

It is what it is. You are fired, and there is nothing you can do about it other than move on to pursuing your next opportunity.

It's their loss. Your ex-employer probably could have been more direct about things you could have done to keep your job, and you would have improved exponentially from that point. It is also likely that they let you go for what most people would consider a stupid reason, but whatever. It is highly unlikely you will ever be fired for the same reason again, and you have learned your lesson.

This process will likely take longer than you think because you are now working on everyone else's schedule. Your urgency does not constitute an emergency for everyone you are looking to for help. Very few people will treat your job search as urgently as you will.

You are going to get rejected a lot. Swallow this pill right now and know that it is simply part of the process. Again, you are going to get rejected a lot. Did I mention you are going to get rejected a lot?

This is all very small in the grand scheme of things. Perhaps the job search takes you an entire year. How tiny is that in the context of a career that might span forty to sixty years? Wouldn't you rather take an additional few months fighting for the opportunity that you want rather than quickly taking the opportunity that is simply available?

Take every piece of advice people give to you with a grain of salt. People will try to steer you in a certain direction because it is what they have seen work in the past or what they want to see for you. Listen to their advice and make your own evaluation as to which parts of their advice you will take and which parts you will reject.

People who give you advice on what to do and where to go will have risk tolerance and patience different from your own.

OK—one motivational phrase…

YOLO (You Only Live Once), my friend. It is a huge cliché, but it is important to keep in mind. Do not live a life full of regret because you failed to even try to pursue the thing that interested you the most.

Think back to all the adversity and failure you have experienced in your life. Are you still breathing? Did it not all come with a silver lining?

Staying positive is important, but there will be times when you will catch yourself thinking negatively, and that is completely OK. Acknowledging from the beginning that there will be inevitable feelings of failure, pain, frustration, and sadness is good because you will have anticipated them, and when they arrive you will have already accepted them as part of the process.

Simply ask yourself why you are having negative thoughts and what you can do to make them stop. Typically "just keeping going" and taking into account the statements in italics above will help you return to equilibrium.

CHAPTER 7

Who Should You Talk To First?

You can really ruin what could be a great start to your job search by speaking with certain people too soon in the process.

The first person you should speak with is someone whom you are close with personally. Let us call them your Special Person. This may be a spouse, a family member, a mentor, or a friend. When you speak with them, let it all out. Being able to go to them in situations like this is the purpose of your relationship with them in the first place, right? Tell them exactly what happened as well as what you are thinking. Be completely honest. Now is not the time to beat around the bush or sugar coat your thoughts and feelings.

Telling all of this to your Special Person will be a relief. You can now move on with your life, and it is likely your Special Person will have some encouraging words or advice for you once you tell them about your experience. Remember to take their advice with a grain of salt, as what they recommend to you may not be what you know truly interests you.

Who exactly are the people I mentioned whom you might speak with too soon and potentially ruin a great start to your transition? They are people from whom you will seek your next job. A big mistake to avoid is going home and firing off your resume to these people as soon as you can. This is the best way to blow great opportunities that might be easier to obtain if you just exercise a little patience.

Why is that a big mistake? The day you got fired, you were given an essentially unlimited amount of time to prepare for the pursuit of your top opportunities. Of course, your financial resources may run out before you run out of time, but you get what I am saying—you at least have some time to prepare. It doesn't sound like a great idea to go home and send off your unrevised resume and risk getting an interview for the next day with little time to prepare. Don't be the eager beaver who collapses the dam, but stay aware of your financial runway.

Let's say you want to get a job at Apple. The first person you should contact is not someone who currently works for Apple. It should not be the Apple hiring manager for your region. You should not apply directly via LinkedIn two hours after you get fired. If you want to get a job at Apple, talk to someone who used to work there but does not anymore. Utilize all the online resources available that talk in great detail about the position that interests you at Apple. Contact your personal network to see if they know anyone who used to work there and if they can connect you to them. Go on LinkedIn and send messages to people who you see used to work there and ask them if they would be willing to offer ten minutes of their time over the phone to tell you about their experience. Ask them about the hiring process and what the company looks for in candidates. Whatever you do, do not make the first person you call someone from the actual company that is at the top of your list of hopeful future employers.

Why is this? Isn't it crazy to resist filling out the application right now when the position might disappear tomorrow?

What I discovered, and what you will hopefully avoid discovering, is that you can absolutely ruin an opportunity by pursuing it too quickly and without doing your homework first. For example, within just a few days of being terminated (what a lovely word they use, right?), I scheduled time to speak with an employer without asking anyone how they might approach an interview with them. I also provided them with a resume that was not designed specifically around why I would be the perfect addition to their team. Needless to say, that one did not work out for me. What if you are the perfect person for the job, but your resume seems to be crafted for a completely different kind of role? You won't even get to interview, because you failed to take the time to make a few easy fixes to your resume. In the next chapter, I will cover tips regarding your resume.

Once word of your termination gets around (people love to gossip, and it will likely spread like wildfire), a lot of people will reach out to you, particularly ex-colleagues who managed to escape the knife, to say how sorry they are, to wish you good luck, and to offer themselves as resources in case you need anything. Do not burn any bridges. Respond quickly and courteously. Thank them, tell them you are optimistic, and make sure to offer yourself as a resource to them as well. Even if that completely phony, ass-kissing colleague who had their career handed to them because they knew how to game the system and slither through office politics reaches out to you, respond to them as if they were your best friend at work. Imagine how much you would beat yourself up if you later met with a hopeful employer who happened to be friends with that person and would rely on them for feedback on whether you would be a good hire. There is only an upside in responding kindly to your ex-colleagues and a lot of potential downsides if you decide to get nasty with them or complain about your circumstances.

Even if you disliked your manager, send them a thank-you email or handwritten note. You will be glad you did as you fill out your next job application and are asked for the contact information of your previous manager or supervisor.

Remember when I talked about listening to your thoughts as you walked, exercised, meditated, or spent time away from your phone for at least the first ten minutes after waking up? It is likely that during those times, you had a lot of questions, and you may have thought of a few people who would be helpful in providing answers to them. There may be just one job or company you have your eye on for your next move, or there may be a plethora of options you would like to explore. Now is the time to set up meetings with people who have previously (not currently!) worked in these roles so you can have a better idea of whether those opportunities would suit you.

Should you talk to headhunters and staffing firms yet? No. Should you talk to hiring managers yet? No.

You need to get your resume on point first. Take a deep breath in through your nose and slowly exhale.

Stay patient.

CHAPTER 8

The Resume

Ahhh, the resume. The resume.

Can you believe that employers put such an immense amount of weight on this piece of paper, when they could learn so much more about you by sitting and having a conversation with you in person?

Unfortunately, the resume is a crucial part of this job-seeking game. One mistake you absolutely must avoid is underestimating the importance of the resume in this process. Perhaps you have forgotten how important it is since you have not touched it up nor had to use it for the last few years.

Your resume is a snapshot of you for your potential employer, so you must make sure it is on point. Unfortunately, the world of "*human* resources" is becoming so digitized that it is likely you will be eliminated by a *computer*, not a human, and might never get a chance to interview, simply because you didn't spend the extra time or money making your resume excellent. Maybe you didn't spend enough time making sure it had all the right key words included so that the computer, or possible human, first line of defense would invite you in to learn more about you.

There are so many people out there competing for the same jobs who are putting together absolutely stellar resumes, even if the reality is that they do not qualify. Their experience actually might not be better than yours, but they may have mastered the art of marketing and embellishing their experience and personal brand. They are like your friend who looks pretty hot on Instagram but is actually hideous.

With this in mind, cater your resume specifically to the opportunity you are chasing. If you plan to apply to different types of roles or industries, then it is a good idea to have different versions of your resume prepared.

What do I mean by having your resume "cater" to different opportunities you are chasing? I am saying you need to customize your resume and emphasize the aspects of your previous experience that you know the hiring manager for a specific role will be seeking. For example, if you are applying for a sales job and in your previous role you were doing a combination of sales and customer service, provide more details on and highlight (not literally) your accomplishments and experience in sales. Specifically, you might want to include language about quotas, sales, business development, goals, targets, and how you met or exceeded them for a sales role.

One thing you should include on your resume that is sort of the "special sauce" as it pertains to hiring these days is how you qualify as a diversity candidate. Many companies are required to or are trying harder to have a diverse workforce. Whether it is because they genuinely think it is important, or they are getting pressure from their shareholders, or they simply fear discrimination lawsuits, companies are putting a huge emphasis on this. Make sure to include anything on your resume that will make you stand out as a diversity candidate and ensure you provide all demographic information about yourself in job applications. This does not just mean diversity pertaining to your demographic characteristics (age, country of origin, etc.), but also your economic diversity and any *adversity* that may set you apart from others. For example, if you spend some of your free time volunteering with an organization that provides financial literacy education because you grew up in a financially difficult environment, make sure you include that volunteer experience on your resume. If you are asked about it, you have a huge opportunity to bond with an interviewer and give them the chance to see the human side of you and learn how you became who you are. Make sure to put things like this on your resume that may bait the interviewer into topics you would like to discuss with them.

Different employers will want to see specific things (like your GPA, certifications, etc.) on your resume depending on the industry, company, or job. I do not want to waste your time outlining all the different strategies for different industries and roles. You will need to use the plethora of online resources to discover what the position you are seeking will value the most on your resume.

Speaking of resources, there are a lot of them out there for helping you put together and perfect your resume or resumes. Before we discuss those resources, here is what you should do:

1. Do research on what is most important to emphasize on a resume for the type of position you are seeking.

2. Look at templates and examples online of resumes for that type of position (it is completely OK, and do not

stress out, if you are not able to find any—I will personally email you templates if you send me a message).

3. Make your best effort to draft your resume (or fill out an existing template) completely on your own.

If you do not have a resume, or would like to start over from scratch, a helpful exercise is to open a blank file on your computer (or take out a blank sheet of paper) and write out your experiences from your previous positions, making sure not to worry about how much space you fill. You can then use that as that "raw data" from which you will create your resume or different versions of your resume.

Keep in mind that the process of making your first resume will likely be pretty grueling and take several hours. Do not get anxious or stressed out if it takes longer than you thought it would. Creating a solid resume is a very labor-intensive and thoughtful process. Don't forget about all those fakers out there who are putting everything they have into their resumes so that they can beat qualified people like you to the interview seat. Don't let them have any advantage over you in this category.

Let's return to all those resources that can help you create and perfect your resume. First, you have the free resources. You really should be able to create a qualified resume utilizing resources online, but again, if you are not at all resourceful, email me and I will provide you with templates.

Once you have created a draft on your own (or not), tap your personal network for help! Ask your friends who are in the industry to take a look at it and provide edits for you. Formatting a resume can be a real bitch, and is unnecessarily time consuming, so you should see if you can get someone to send you a copy of their resume so you can delete their content and fill in the blanks with your own. This is hands down the easiest way to develop a resume. Do not try to reinvent the wheel and format the resume all on your own, as doing this will drive you crazy. Make sure you ask very politely for their help and let them know you are grateful (you should genuinely be extremely grateful, but make sure to let them know). Also make sure to let them know exactly what your goal is so they don't feel as though they are wasting your time or feel they are in a position where they are being asked to decide for you.

Beyond your free resources, you have some paid resources as well. There is a high degree of variability in terms of price and quality in the world of professional resume writers, so be very careful. Please note, you should not feel guilty or bad for paying someone to write a resume for you. It is not cheating. Writing a resume absolutely sucks, and it is unlikely something you practice, so it may be more efficient to just have someone hammer out that first draft for you for a couple hundred bucks. If you go this route, try to find one that has online reviews, and ensure you can speak with a human and have a consultation before considering paying for their services.

On your computer, create several carefully labeled folders for different versions of your resume. Save each version as both a Word document and a PDF. If you convert a Word document into a PDF file, you absolutely must open the PDF to make sure it didn't convert strangely (sometimes it will be a one-page Word document, but when you convert it to a PDF it will be more than one page).

Name the resume files on your computer in such a way that they show you are organized and thorough. For example, you might want to name it something like **John_Smith_Resume_06.13.2019.** To whomever you are sending your resume, automatically and subtly you are sending a message that you are organized. Make sure not to call it something like **John_Smith_Edit33_SalesVersion**, as you will be showing the employer that you have different versions of your resume and may not even be sure of what you want to do with your life. When you send copies of your resume to potential employers, always send in PDF format unless asked otherwise!

CHAPTER 9

Who Should You Talk To Second?

Now that you have perfected your resume, you are permitted to talk to a few new groups of people.

First, you may speak with headhunters and other people whose job it is to place employees into companies. Be open and honest with these people and be very specific about which opportunities you would like to pursue. Do not let them convince you to do something that does not interest you. Not only is that bad for you in the long term, but it will confirm to them that you are weak and desperate. You're not.

Headhunters are paid to place people into specific opportunities and may try to steer you in a direction that does not interest you. Politely decline any opportunities they mention that do not interest you and tell them what you want as precisely as you can. Do not break your relationship and ongoing dialogue with them when you realize they do not have anything that interests you when you first speak. Whatever you told them you are seeking may become available two months from your first conversation, when it is highly likely you will still be on the hunt. Another thing to keep in mind is that headhunters are humans, and you should treat them like potential employers. Be polite and polished when you speak with them over the phone or over email. If you meet with them, dress professionally. It reflects well on you, and they will be much more likely to introduce you to potential employers if they personally think you are a good candidate.

The first thing these headhunters will ask you for is your resume. When they do, you will be glad you put in all the work perfecting it before you reached out to them.

Feel free to contact as many headhunters as you wish. The more horses you have in the race, the higher your likelihood of winning.

It is possible your employer provided you with outplacement service firms to assist you in your transition. In my experience, these outplacement firms have not been helpful and have delivered subpar quality services. It is likely that your company went bottom-dollar on their budget for outplacement services for employees they terminated. Makes sense, right? Be careful attending events or working with the consultants of outplacement service firms. If you use a lot of their services, you may start to feel like it is their duty to find you your next opportunity, when in reality the responsibility is yours completely. Figure out which services they offer that may be helpful to you and only use those. They may have people who will help you construct your resume, and they may provide job bulletins with relevant opportunities. If they provide you with an outplacement services consultant to handle your "case," certainly take the time to tell them about what you are looking for and move on with your efforts. Do not rely solely on this person to help you with your career transition. Again, more horses in the race.

You may now reach out to current employees of companies that have jobs you would like to pursue, but not before you do one more thing. Make sure you have a thorough understanding of the job description you would like to discuss with these people. In a later chapter I will outline the information you should know before you reach out to employers or interview. You will be glad you waited until this point to make contact with them.

Now is the part where you put on your stalker hat. You have to get onto the radar of the people who you want to hire you. Be careful before attempting to contact anyone directly, as there could be precise instructions on their posted job descriptions to not contact them through any means other than those they specify. Find those people who you feel will either be able to help you get more information on the role you are pursuing and/or may have some influence in the decision-making process. First, see if they are connected with anyone you know on LinkedIn. If anyone you know is connected with them, ask your contact for an introduction. Otherwise, look for their contact information on the company website and their LinkedIn profile. If you are still unable to get any contact information for them, send them an invitation and message on LinkedIn.

If you are up for a little trial and error, try to figure out the company's email formula and send an email directly to the person with whom you would like to connect. For instance, if you see online that the email for the secretary, John Doe, is Jdoe@company.com, it is highly likely that the Jane Smith you are trying to reach can be reached at Jsmith@company.com. When you reach out to these individuals, simply tell them about the specific opportunity within their company that interests you and ask if they would have time to talk with you about their experience. Make your email thorough so that you can reduce the amount of back and forth between you and this person. For example:

jsmith@companyxyz.com

Availability

Hi Jane,

I hope this message finds you well. I came across your profile because I am interested in the Operations Manager position with Company XYZ and see that you have worked in Operations for over 5 years.

Would you have time for a brief phone call next week? I am hoping to learn more about the position before I apply so that I do not waste your time.

If so, please let me know which of the following times would work for you, as well as the best number where I can reach you, and I will send a calendar invitation:

Tuesday, June 18th
10:00am
2:00pm

Wednesday, June 19th
9:00am
2:00pm

Thank you in advance for your time.

With kind regards,
Marc Schaevitz
Cell: 555.555.5555

There are a few elements of this email that need to be highlighted. First, as I mentioned, it is thorough. It enables you to accomplish everything you want in one email, and it makes life easiest on your recipient. In this one email, you stated your purpose for reaching out, you extended an invitation to connect over the phone, provided potential times to speak, asked for the recipient's contact number (if they prefer to call you, they will likely mention that, and you have already provided them with your phone number in the signature), and made very clear who would put the meeting on the calendar once you establish a time. All your recipient needs to do now is respond with a time and a preference for who will call whom.

While you are sending out invitations to connect, you may also start filling out applications for positions that interest you. Make sure everything you enter into your job applications is consistent with the content of your resume AND with reality. You know what would suck? If you thought it would look better to say you worked somewhere for two years instead of one year and nine months, and then your potential new employer called your old employer to verify your dates of employment only to discover that you were dishonest. Don't lie. This applies to your GPA, number of sales you made, number of articles you published, or any other historical data that has to do with your experience or performance. It applies to everything.

If the applications you are filling out have open-ended questions that require you to type out long answers, create a document on your computer where you will compose those answers prior to copying and pasting them into online applications. Not only will this save you from the devastating consequences of losing your internet connection while filling out those applications, but it will also enable you to access those answers for future applications so that you can save time. Have a friend check your drafted answers for grammatical, spelling, and contextual errors. Spell check it on your own before you send it to your friend. Many potential employers will throw away your application if they discover a spelling error, even if the overall message is exactly what the potential employer is seeking. Other information you should type out or write down and have handy from the start is listed below. If you collect all this information over the course of one day and save it for every time you are asked for it, you will save a tremendous amount of time. Wouldn't you prefer to write all this out one time rather than look it up for every application you complete?

1. Name of every company where you have worked over the last ten years, including:

    a. Your start date

    b. Your end date

    c. Your title

    d. The address of your employer

    e. The name of your manager or supervisor

    f. Your manager or supervisor's telephone number and email address

    g. A description of what you did there

2. Name of all schools you have attended, including:

    a. Start date

    b. Graduation date

    c. School address

    d. GPA—it is worth the extra effort to check your transcript (call the school and request for it to be sent to you if you don't have it) to ensure you have the exact value

I will cover how to prepare for the meetings and interviews that you get as a result of those outreaches and applications in later chapters. I will also cover how to conduct yourself during them.

CHAPTER 10

Phone Call, Coffee, Phone Call, Lunch, Lunch, Coffee, Lunch, Breakfast

The title of this chapter is essentially how your weeks should look while you are unemployed. Your calendar should be full of phone calls, coffees, lunch meetings, breakfast meetings, and more phone calls. All of these should be in some way connected to landing your next job. Perhaps they are with hiring managers. Perhaps they are with your friends, who can introduce you to people who are hiring. Perhaps they are with people who used to work for the company where you are trying to land your next job. Perhaps they are with headhunters. Perhaps they are with people who help you collect your thoughts and eliminate opportunities from your job search because they know you well enough to be able to tell when you are not interested in something even when you have not realized it yourself. Perhaps they are with people who are sitting down with you to help you tweak your resume.

Make sure you are perceived as being extremely sharp, punctual, and thorough when you are setting meetings with these people. People who are potentially making introductions have their reputations at stake if they introduce someone in their network to someone lousy. Make them as confident as possible that they are introducing someone who is awesome. How do you do this? A couple simple things:

1. Once you agree on a time and a place to meet or speak over the phone, send a calendar invitation with the date, time, location, and title of your meeting. Make life as easy as possible on this person. Remember, if you send the calendar invitation after confirming meeting details, it is much harder for them to bail on you. This set of actions also makes you look like a better potential employee by showing you are organized, detail-oriented, and can make life easier on others.

2. Do not forget to provide them with anything they ask you for, and do not wait too long to provide it to them. For example, if they say, "Sure, I would be happy to meet with you—send me your resume," you need to send it as soon as you possibly can. If you forget to send your resume to that person, you can pretty much forget about ever getting that introduction or recommendation. Whatever methods you have established for remembering things (to-do lists, reminders on your phone, sending yourself emails, etc.), make sure you use them full force.

3. Show up early. Leave three times as much cushion as you normally would to ensure you arrive on time. This goes for every meeting you have, regardless of whether it is with a hiring manager or a friend who may provide an introduction. Remember, this person is doing you a favor, and/or you are asking them for a job. Show

some respect and gratitude through your punctuality and preparation.

4. Speaking of gratitude, make sure you thank the person you meet with for their help or consideration. Gratefulness goes a very long way, especially if it is genuine.

5. Dress nicely. I am not saying you have to wear a suit and tie to get coffee with an acquaintance who may be able to introduce you to a job opportunity, but dress professionally and don't show up looking too casual. For interviews, again, this is industry specific, and you will need to search online for what is appropriate for your specific industry.

6. Follow up with the person with whom you met. I cover this in the chapter on interviewing, but you should make it a habit to do this after every meeting. Send an email thanking the person you met with for their time and provide them with any materials they requested.

Always stay hedged. Let me explain what I mean if you are not already familiar with the concept of being "hedged." Being hedged just means protecting yourself against potential bad outcomes. If you own a car and you buy car insurance, you are hedging. If you are betting on one team in a championship game, you can hedge by also putting some money on that team's opponent.

Staying hedged in the job game means constantly having multiple different opportunities that you are chasing at any point in time. Do not, under any circumstances, put all your effort into just one position you are seeking. Not only are you setting yourself up for potential disaster if you do not get that job offer, but you will also have lost the opportunity to appear patient to other potential employers if their hiring processes take some time. It may seem odd, but you should feel just as busy, if not busier, while you are unemployed as when you were working. Getting a new job is a full-time job.

Once you have all these meetings set on your calendar, there are some key things you must do to make the most out of them, which I will cover in the following chapters.

CHAPTER 11

How To Tell Potential Employers Why You Got Fired

The thought of telling people you got fired is probably one of the most daunting and stressful things on your mind right now, other than the uncertainty surrounding when you will land your next job.

You should have already gotten some practice telling your Special Person about how and why you were fired (or at least the reason for which your employer *told* you they fired you). It is likely that you told your Special Person the no-frills, honest, full-length version of the story with the addition of your own commentary throughout. If you tell that full-length story to a potential employer, with your commentary included, you are likely to turn them off and make them focus exclusively on your termination as opposed to why you might be a good fit for their team. When speaking with potential employers, you will want to make sure that you keep your story completely honest, but you must tell an abridged version so you can avoid shifting the focus of the entire conversation. Remember, you are there to discuss why you would be a great candidate, not to have an hour-long discussion about your termination. I will elaborate more in a tiny bit.

I want to reemphasize making sure you keep your story completely honest. It is OK to omit details of the story behind your termination, as long as the omitted details don't take away from the truthfulness of the story. Here are the reasons why:

1. It is simply the right thing to do.

2. Being dishonest typically gets you into trouble.

3. You are screwed if your story is not consistent with the story that your previous employer will tell your potential employer when they are asked about the nature of your departure. Someone from the hiring company may just contact one of your former colleagues to try to confirm your story as well.

4. Your potential employer will actually appreciate your honesty. It is highly likely that whomever you are speaking with either has been fired before or knows someone close to them or someone they respect who has been fired at some point in their career. Even if they do not fall into any of these categories, it is likely they have done something, or something has happened in their life, of which they are not proud. You will be rewarded for your honesty.

Let's talk more about how to deliver the message. First, remember that you do not have to discuss your story unless you are asked about it. If your potential employer asks you nothing but questions about why you want to work for them, there is no need to say, "By the way, I got fired —you want to know the story?!" However, if the potential employer incorrectly assumes that you are still working for your previous employer, or assumes that you left on your own initiative, you must correct them. For instance, if they ask you "Why did you quit?" you must correct them and say something along the lines of "I was actually asked to leave, and I am happy to explain why if you would like me to do that." If you are lucky, maybe they will say there is no need to explain and they appreciate your honesty. Similarly, if they give you a clue that they think you are still working, such as saying, "Tell me about what you currently do at Company XYZ," you must tell them you no longer work there as of whatever date you were dismissed. This doesn't mean you have to immediately say you were fired, but they will likely ask you why you are no longer working there.

This is the part where you tell them exactly what happened, but in a tightly packaged way. The most important thing other than keeping your story honest is that you say what you learned from it and how it made you better. For example, you may have been fired for poor performance. In this case, you might say that you agree that your performance was subpar, you have done a lot of reflection on how you could have performed better, and you are prepared to take what you have learned into your next role to make you an even better performer. There are so many different reasons for which you could have been fired and what your takeaways could be, so I am not going into all those lessons. I am sure as you are reading this you are thinking of exactly what you could say.

As mentioned, do not lie or fabricate your story. Trust me, your risk will be far greater if you lie about what happened than if you just tell the truth. You will be valued and rewarded for your honesty over the long term. If someone eliminates you from the hiring process because of your story, that is not someone for whom you want to work, as it is an indicator that they may be too judgmental, non-forgiving, or just arrogant.

Watch your body language and your tone as you discuss why you were fired. If you stutter, hesitate, fidget, or abandon your eye contact as you tell your story, you may be perceived as dishonest. Tell the story with confidence and think of it not as a failure that will stop you from succeeding, but as a springboard for your next step, because that is what it is. Practice telling your story to your Special Person, your dog, or the mirror on your wall.

CHAPTER 12

The Three P's: Prepare, Package, Practice

I am going to provide you with nothing but practical advice in this section that I guarantee will increase your odds of landing the next job.

Some of the information I am telling you to prepare may seem simple, but it is harder to deliver in person than you think. Do not skip this section, as it is probably the most important of all.

For any opportunity where you earn an interview, look up and remember the information that follows. Do not be intimidated, as this is all stuff that can be easily found online and prepared in a very short amount of time.

1. Name of the owner, founder, or co-founders

2. Name of the CEO, co-CEOs, or president (sometimes will be the same as the founder)

3. Name of the leadership team of the division of the company where you are applying or interviewing (for example, if you are interviewing for a position in technology, you should know the name of the CTO)

4. Company history (date the company was founded, a brief summary of the company's history)

5. What the company does. If it has many different functions, know a little about each of them, but know the most about the division where you are applying.

6. Number of employees at the company

7. Location of company headquarters

8. Number of global offices the company has

9. If the company is a for-profit corporation, you need to know how the company makes money and stays alive. How are you supposed to help them make money if you don't even know how they do it?

10. If the company is a non-profit corporation, where does its funding come from?

11. Is the company a public or private company? How big is it in terms of revenues? If it is a publicly traded company, when was its IPO, and what is the current price per share?

12. The exact title of the job for which you are interviewing. It is very possible that the person interviewing you is interviewing people for several different positions. It's not a good look if they ask you and you don't know the exact title.

13. The role, function, and duties of the position for which you are applying.

14. Any recent news on the company. Just do a quick Google search of the company name and read the first three articles.

15. If applying for a blue-collar position, know about one of the company's products, services, or recently completed projects.

16. The name of at least one of the company's clients

If you are armed with the preceding information, you will be a step ahead of most of your competing candidates already. Make sure that for each of the above pieces of information, you have a neatly packaged answer. For example, if you read about the company in the news, have a one- or two-sentence summary of the content, but do not attempt to memorize minute details. For the history of the company, don't try to memorize every major milestone, but rather pick three or four times in its history that you feel are important.

Now, let's take it to the next level.

If you know with whom you will be interviewing ahead of time, do research on that person. Are you worried they will find it creepy that you did research on them? I can't guarantee they will not, but they should not, and it is unlikely. It is 2019. There is more information available on you out there as you read this now than you even know. If you look up this person in advance, it actually sends a message that you take pride in preparation and due diligence. The best two sources of information you should use to research your interviewers beforehand are their company website and LinkedIn. Do NOT look them up on Instagram, Facebook, or any other social media platform. That is crossing the line. Important information to collect includes their career history, where they are originally from, where they went to school, and their involvement in any organizations outside of work.

I will talk in the next section about how to use this research to your advantage.

The objective of doing this research is to find some common ground with the person you meet. It is completely normal if you say you saw something on their LinkedIn profile and are interested in hearing more about it. It is likely they will think you are more invested in them and the opportunity if you took the time to do research beforehand. They probably also looked you up before you met. If you come to them knowing their basic career history, you can have a deeper conversation by asking more specific questions.

What you should NOT do with the information you know about this person is act like you do not know it and then bait them into talking about it. For example, if you know for a fact that they went to school in New York City, don't try to indirectly get them to talk about it by asking them if they have ever been there. Doing things like that will crush you.

Quiz yourself on all the information you've researched on the company, as well as any information you researched on the person you've planned to meet with, as if you were preparing for an exam. You should be able to mentally retrieve all of it instantly as you are speaking so your conversations are smooth.

What we have covered so far in this chapter has taken you through the details of how to prepare and package information in your head prior to meeting with your interviewers. In the next section, I will let you in on all the questions I have been asked in interviews, other common interview questions, and interview questions I have asked candidates myself when responsible for hiring new employees.

CHAPTER 13

Interviewing: Key Pieces of Advice That Have Been Proven To Work

You are much more likely to land that job if you nail the interview. Do not overthink this process. There are four things you must do successfully in order to have an excellent interview:

1. Build rapport with your interviewer.

2. Be prepared.

3. Be genuine.

4. Follow up.

Let's cover these in order. Think of an interview as a first date. You should strive to make that first impression as smooth and not awkward as possible. For that person to like you, trust you, and want to spend more time with you in the future, you must build rapport with them. Remember: Not only must this person think you are adequately skilled or trainable for the job, but they also must at least be OK with seeing you on a nearly daily basis.

Side note: There are a lot of free resources online that cover dress and etiquette (how hard to shake the interviewer's hand, when to wear a tie, how to sit, etc.) for interviews, which I will not cover. This is industry specific, and I encourage you to utilize the power of Google for this. If you are still not able to find any good websites for tips on this for your specific industry or situation, please visit my website, where I have posted some links:

www.ShitIGotFired.com

The following is a set of tips and steps to guide you on your first interview. This information is derived from interviews I have conducted and experienced over the course of over a decade.

1. Bring a pen and notebook with you to the interview. In your notepad, have three to five shortened versions of questions you will ask written down that pertain to the job and/or company. You will ask these at the end of the interview. Asking them will show you have given thought to the position and that you are invested. Do not bring any questions that have answers available online already. Don't try to memorize the questions word for word. Just know what they are generally. As mentioned, in your notepad, you can write down shortened versions or just one word that will remind you of the questions. For example, if you want to ask something like "How would you describe the company culture here?" just write down "culture" in your notepad.

2. Before you start your meeting, go to a bathroom and make sure you do not have anything in your teeth or on your face, and make sure your hair didn't get crazy on the way there.

3. Before you meet your interviewer, if there is a recep-
   tionist, secretary, or assistant who helps you to your
   meeting room or helps you get situated, you must
   make sure to be kind and polite to this person.
   Introduce yourself to them and offer a handshake. Ask
   them how their day is going. Who knows what kind
   of influence they may have in the decision-making
   process? Perhaps they are a relative of the interviewer
   or they are your interviewer's manager and they are
   filling in for the secretary who is out sick. Perhaps they
   are a relative of the founder of the company and there
   is no chance you would get a job if you were anything
   but honey to that person.

4. Do not be afraid to accept a water or coffee if it is
   offered to you. Remember: You need to be genuine.
   Just don't forget to be extremely polite when it is
   offered to you, as well as when you receive it. If you're
   thirsty, accept a water.

5. After you say hello, shake hands, and introduce
   yourself by name to your interviewer, show gratitude.
   Simply thank them for making the time to see you and
   consider you.

6. Now comes the part where you must be smooth. If it
   is a Monday, ask them if they had a nice weekend. If it
   is a Thursday or Friday, ask them how their week has
   been. If it is a Tuesday or Wednesday, ask them how
   their week is going. This opens up the conversation to
   focus on your interest in them, and it is open-ended

enough that they can choose whatever is top of mind for them. Make sure to be prepared with an answer when they ask you the same question!

7. Slow down your speaking, and don't be afraid to pause for silence to make sure the other person is finished speaking. If you speak too quickly, you will show you are nervous, you will be more likely to fumble your words, you will stress out your interviewer, and you will appear less confident. Try to practice for this by speaking a few notches slower in conversations with everyone outside of interviews.

8. Prepare your answers to potential interview questions. I will cover these next.

You must come to the interview prepared to answer a wide variety of questions. I have been interviewed many times and also have conducted many interviews. Similar to dress code, interview questions are typically industry specific, so you will need to use the power of the internet to search for additional common questions that may be asked for the job you are pursuing. I would be doing you a disservice by providing you with a bunch of interview questions to prepare for that you will definitely not be asked. Some interviews may include case studies, situational questions (for example, "What would you do in this situation…?"), riddles, or even quirky questions like "If you were an animal, what kind of animal would you be, and why?" Again, use the power of the internet to see what people were asked in previous interviews. Use that information to think of other questions that may be asked and prepare answers to those as well. You can also get some of this information from the network of people with whom you had all your coffees and lunch meetings.

Another thing you will want to be extremely familiar with is the content of your resume. It is likely your interviewer will have your resume in front of them as they interview you and will look to it to generate questions. Be prepared to go into detail about any aspect of your resume when you are asked by your interviewer to tell them a little more about it. For example, know your GPA, and be prepared to tell them a little more about exactly how you "improved processes" or "leveraged resources." If you say you are a great cold caller, you better be ready to do a roleplay with your interviewer.

Let's look at a few potential interview questions. Whether or not you expect to be asked these questions, they will be important to know and rehearse. Some of the questions are used to quickly eliminate people from the interview process. For example, a simple question may be, "What do you know about what we do?" If you are not able to answer this question with accuracy, you are gone. See more examples of questions and commands here:

1. *Tell me about yourself.* How long and to what extent of detail you will want to go with this question is industry specific. One thing you will want to make sure to do is tie the end of your answer smoothly into why you are sitting in your seat interviewing with this company.

2. *Can you tell me more about this experience on your resume...?* Remember to know everything on both your resume and your LinkedIn page so that you are able to elaborate on any of the content.

3. *What exactly did you do at (previous job or company)?*

4. *Why did you leave your previous job?* You should be ready for this one. Already covered it for an entire chapter.

5. *What do you know about what we do?*

6. *Can you tell me what you know about the history of this company?*

7. *What role are you interviewing for?*

8. *Why our company?* Here, make sure you can explain why you like their company, particularly why you like their company over their competitors. It is a pretty safe bet to mention that you have met or spoken with people who used to work there and heard great things about the culture and quality of the people. Just make sure you actually did meet with people and learned those things.

9. *Where do you see yourself in X years?* This is a VERY important question that can make or break your success in getting the job. They may ask this question in the context of five, ten, or fifteen years. Have an answer ready for all of them. If what you tell them you envision for yourself in five years is something that would not be possible at their company or in the role for which you are applying, it will hurt you, unless the position is marketed as only lasting for a certain period of time. People will want to hire you and invest

in your success if your vision for yourself is possible within their company in the future.

10. *What do you like about the role you are interviewing for?*

11. *What do you know about the role you are interviewing for?*

12. *Why should we choose you?*

Do not be afraid to ask your interviewer for clarification on a term or an acronym. If you just smile and nod the entire time that they are talking about something with which you are not familiar, you are at risk of portraying yourself as a person who is afraid to ask questions, and they will not want to hire you. Further, if you risk saying you are familiar with a term with which you are actually not familiar, and they then ask you to explain it, you are screwed, and you will not be hired. You are a liar.

You should have answers prepared to all of the preceding questions, plus answers to all of the questions you researched on your own time that are industry, company, or job specific. You should type or write them out and practice answering them, but you should NOT try to memorize them. If you do, you are putting yourself in a bad position in the event that a question is similar to one of the questions you anticipated, but not quite the same. It will be very hard to modify an answer that you memorized word-for-word. Also, if you try to memorize the answers, it will usually be detectable by your interviewer. If you forget part of the memorized answer as you are reciting it to your interviewer, you may stumble over your words and stress out over omitting something that you meant to include.

With this being said, just have a few bullet points for answers to all of the questions you've determined are likely to be asked.

Remember to be genuine. You want to be hired for who you are. If you are trying too hard to act like someone you are not in an interview, you will sound robotic, people will be able to tell you are not genuine, and you will miss out on opportunities to form genuine connections with your interviewer. Do not be ashamed to talk about your quirks or hobbies (maybe keep your interest in weekend swinger parties confidential, though), as your candor will be appreciated, and you should make sure you feel comfortable being yourself from the start.

Along these same lines, do not be afraid to talk about anything that makes you special or unique, especially as it pertains to your diversity and/or adversity. Try your absolute hardest to tie your diversity and/or adversity into an answer to any one of the questions posed. It will likely be one of the more memorable things your interviewer will recall from your time together.

Once your interview is complete, make sure to thank your interviewer again. If they have not already volunteered the information, it is appropriate to ask them when you might expect to hear from them next. If you want to be more aggressive and in control, you can ask them when would be a good time for you to follow up with them. Of course, if they give you a specific date, you better follow up with them exactly on that date—no sooner, no later.

Finally, make sure to follow up with every one of your interviewers by email. You will want to make sure you do this no later than the end of the same day that you had the interview or interviews. If you are stuck on what to include in your follow-up email, there are endless templates online. If you are still stuck on which template to use for your follow-up email, and the internet is not providing enough, just send me an email, and I will provide you with a template.

CHAPTER 14

More Special Sauce...

There is one more drop of special sauce in this process that will set you apart from other candidates.

Sometimes a potential employer will ask for personal and/or professional references later in the interview process once they have screened you a bit. You can give yourself a massive advantage over other candidates by *proactively* asking your personal and professional connections to write and send recommendations to your potential employer. For example, have your former manager email a recommendation to the hiring manager where you are interviewing before the hiring manager asks you to provide recommendations.

Make life easy on the people you reach out to for references and tell them you would be happy to draft the recommendations for them if they choose so that all they have to do is copy and paste from their email.

CHAPTER 15

Things Will Definitely Start To Look Up, And When They Do, Here's What You Should Do

Everything is going to suck at the beginning, and it will be stressful, especially once that feeling of freedom from your last job fades. It is acceptable to not feel great about your position in life once you get fired, but that feeling will ebb, and you will land your next job. It is just a matter of time, patience, dedication, preparation, and persistence. You also must remember that you are valuable, and everyone should want you to join their team.

Some people catch lucky breaks and already have their next thing lined up when they get fired. Some people find their next job within a week. Their dad knows everyone at the yacht club. They were there for someone during rough times. For others, it can take months, or even over a year, especially if they refuse to take jobs simply because they are easy to acquire.

After you get fired, you will experience periods of low activity or high rejection, but you will also experience the relief of finally landing a job, and you will need to prepare for the possibility that you may have several options in front of you.

If you get an offer, pay attention to the date by which you must accept or reject it. It would be a shame to miss an opportunity because you forgot to sign a piece of paper or send a confirmatory email.

A verbal offer is worthless. Do not go parading around town telling everyone about the job you just landed after receiving a verbal offer. Wait until you have that contract in hand to tell someone you received an offer.

If you receive an offer from Company A, but you want a job with Company B, you must navigate very carefully. If you tell Company B that you received an offer from Company A and are thinking about taking it, but you are still not sure whether you would like to work for Company A or Company B, you completely blew your chance with Company B. The proper way to play this is to tell Company B that you received an offer from Company A, but you would much prefer to work for Company B. If they are interested at all in hiring you and fear losing you to Company A, they will really speed things up at that point and/or try to match or beat your other offer in some way (salary, benefits, title, etc.).

There are numerous resources (even entire books) available on negotiating salaries, and I encourage you to refer to them if you arrive at a point where you think you deserve more money.

I wrote this book because, after I got fired and landed my next job, I was told by many people that I had navigated the process well. I wanted to make sure that others could benefit from the strategies I used, the mistakes I made, and the lessons I learned along the way.

My hope is that this book has given you a sense of direction and structure as you pursue your next opportunity, and that you can point to it as a reason why you were able to land your next job.